Pig Chinese Horoscope 2023

By
IChingHun FengShuisu

Table of Contents

Introduce

The character of people born in the year of the PIG

People born in this year are wise, trustworthy, kind-hearted, generous, and selfless. It's not a big deal if whoever sees it loves and gets along with others easily. You are cautious, attentive, and brave; try to put your trust in me. You'll know they're so good at doing everything right and never disappointing you. People born in the Year of the Pig are universally adored. People born in this year are born to serve and to give. The majority of people take advantage of this opportunity. Even as they get older, people born in the Year of the Pig don't feel bad about it. People born in the Year of the Pig continue to believe that everyone is born with a good heart. People born in this year are willing to forego their happiness to be good friends who value manners. People who do not know people born in the Year of the Pig well may believe they are unethical. And she enjoys eating chocolate after dinner, which she always overdoes. People born in this year are sensitive, sweet, innocent, affectionate, romantic, and occasionally jealous.

Strength:
People born in the Year of the Pig are gentle, forgiving, and unconcerned about minor issues.

Weaknesses:
People born in this year tend to trust people who are easy to follow and do not have their ideas.

Love:
People born in this year are charming and serious about everything, but they are not as sincere in love as they should be. You like people all over the place, and if you like someone, you'll have to flirt with them. The good-looking kind Please do not approach me. In marriage and love, a woman born in the Year of the Pig outperforms a man. That is, if you meet your true soul mate, you should leave. The young woman will not waste herself or her heart for anyone other than the young pig. Will not stop there, as a result, finding a serious

person can be difficult. Ancient texts say that most women born in the Year of the Pig tend to have a younger partner.

Suitable Career:
People born in this year are charming and serious about everything, but they are not as sincere in love as they should be. You like people all over the place, and if you like someone, you'll have to flirt with them. The good-looking kind Please do not approach me. In marriage and love, a woman born in the Year of the Pig outperforms a man. That is, if you meet your true soul mate, you should leave. The young woman will not waste herself or her heart for anyone other than the young pig. Will not stop there, as a result, finding a serious person can be difficult. Ancient texts say that most women born in the Year of the Pig tend to have a younger partner.

Year of the PIG (Fire) | (1947) & (2007)

"The PIG is on its way" is a person born in the year of the PIG at the age of 76 years (1947) and 16 years (2007)

Overview

The "Shackle Star" is the planet that will orbit his destiny this year for the 76-year-old Senior Lord. Its influence will entangle you in chaos until you are unable to escape. As a result, before taking action in any work, you should look carefully. Today is the time to find an heir to take over the work and relieve the burden. Even with a lot of experience, no activity can be impatient. However, today's bodies are incapable of doing so as soon as the mind commands. As a result, having an heir or an assistant to take over, as well as your experience analyzing matters, is advantageous. Trade jobs will continue to expand. The main issue this year is your health because the fated house has experienced two orbiting evil stars, "Dao Khuang Sor" (Dow Chains) and "Dao Noor Sing" (Danger Planet), which frequently directly affect unforeseen events such as chaos that robs families of peace and accidents. In addition, illnesses such as gastritis, joint pain, headache, and blood pressure disease will be infested. As a result, if you notice any unusual symptoms, you should see a doctor right away, control your diet, find time to exercise lightly and avoid stress.

The planet that orbits the zodiac this year is the "snare star" for the young destiny of the Year of the Pig, around the age of 16. (Danger planet). Everything was not going so well this year. Education must be more diligent than ever before. Activities and other extraneous tasks Please do not disregard safety. Children should be warned to be cautious in their activities, including risky travel. Be wary of unexpected events and take precautions to avoid injury from accidents.

Career and Business

On the job, things are moving slowly, but there is still progress. What you should remember is to not rush into major decisions and to think carefully before acting. Be wary of conflicts, especially those bound by legal contracts, as well as personnel management, switching positions, and duties. Especially the months that do not support you, such as the 1st month of China (4 Feb. – 5 Mar.), the 4th month of China (6 May – 5 June), the 7th month of China (8 Aug. – 7 Sep.) and the 10th month of China (7 Nov – 6 Dec). Work will face challenges during these months. Keep an eye out for internal agency protests. Take care not to deliver the work on time because an intervention will cause damage. You have the right to be duped into increasing the granularity of reviewing contract terms by entering into a contract of employment or employment. Furthermore, you should not increase your investment because you have the right to be duped. Finding a trusted heir or descendant to assist in taking over the work is the best option. And you must let go and rely on the next generation to manage.

For the month that your work and investment have a bright and prosperous direction, such as the 2nd month of China (6 Mar. – 4 Apr.), the 6th month of China (7 Jul. – 7 Aug.), the 8th month of China (8 Sep. – 7 Oct.) and 9th month of China (8 Oct. – 6 Nov.) is another good time to find heirs to continue working or to assist with investment management. Taking care of all branch operations will result in handsome profits.

Financial

Fortune-telling is considered moderate, although fortune is sufficient. But if you are too greedy, it can be damaged. The best way this year is to save money and not be superfluous. And plan your finances carefully to avoid problems later. Especially during months of financial congestion, including unexpected expenditures, such as the 1st month of China (4 Feb. – 5 Mar.)., the 4th month of China (6 May – 5 Jun.). , 7th month of China (8 Aug. – 7 Sep.) and the 10th month of China (7 Nov. – 6 Dec.) Gambling and gambling are prohibited. Allow others to borrow money or sign financial guarantees on your behalf. Don't put your money into illegal ventures. Be wary of potentially fraudulent investments.

For the months that your finances will be smooth: 2nd month of China (6 Mar. – 4 Apr.)., the 6th month of China (7 Jul. – 7 Aug.), 8th month of China (8 Sep. – 7 Oct.), and the 9th month of China (8 Oct. – 6 Nov.).

Family

Although this year may bring good news and an auspicious event, it is still influenced by the evil stars that invade. This frequently leads to arguments and conflicts among family members, resulting in a lack of peace in the home. Especially accidents that may occur to people who are insane. Family members may be duped or influenced to become involved in a lawsuit to cause trouble. You must exercise caution during the mourning of elderly relatives. Especially during the months when the family will have chaos, such as the 1st month of China (4 Feb. – 5 Mar.), the 4th month of China (6 May – 5 Jun.), the 7th month of China (8 Aug. – 7 Sep) and the 10th month of China (7 Nov. – 6 Dec.) Increase safety precautions and pay more attention to people's health in the home. Be wary of minors or attendants who are arguing. Be wary of damaged, lost, or stolen valuables.

You will find friends to give you good advice and help if you have relatives who are in good health. You will also be able to go on excursions or organize merit-making activities, and charity events or volunteer to help victims or make public benefits together.

Love
This year's teenage fortune will be supported solely by adult lovers. As a result, for those who meet him to be compassionate, one should behave well and maintain humility. and will be the people's love center in the house

The senior destiny should act appropriately and be the primary figure for the younger so that the children can be respected and not float around in different orbits. Because there could be issues that cause you to lose your respectability. Any action should be mentally restrained to cut off the fire at the source. So you don't end up getting involved in unsolvable problems later. But be careful during the month when the love of the destiny of the two age cycles will cause arguments. Conflicts occurred: 1st month of China (4 Feb. – 5 Mar.), 4th month of China (6 May – 5 Jun.), the 7th month of China (8 Aug. – 7 Sep.), and the 10th month of China (7 Nov. – 6 Dec.).

Health

Despite being healthy by age, be aware of diseases related to the gastrointestinal tract, allergies, and various infectious diseases for the fate of adolescence. Be cautious when driving and working with machine tools.

When it comes to the Elder Fates, you must be extra cautious about your health. Because the body is weak this year, eating must be restricted. Keep an eye out for intestinal diseases, diabetes, and high blood pressure. because the house of fate has evil stars that snare and snare If you suspect that something is wrong with your body, please consult a doctor for a diagnosis and treatment. Especially during the month when Chao Chakha in both age cycles need to take care of their health closely, namely the 1st month of China (4 Feb.

– 5 Mar.), the 4th month of China (6 May – 5 Jun)., in the 7th month of China (8 Aug. – 7 Sep.) and in the 10th month of China (7 Nov. – 6 Dec.) to be vigilant, if sickness occurs, they should be treated promptly and beware of the dangers of mourning for elders.

Year of the PIG (Earth) | (1959)

" The PIG traverses the mountain" is a person born in the year of the PIG at the age of 64 years (1959)

Overview

Lord destiny around the age of 64 years because the planet orbiting into your destiny house this year is "Dao Nuang Sing" (Planet Danger) The family is smooth and bright even this year. The children's home will receive auspicious energy. There will be positive news. There will be happy happenings in the house. New growth opportunities will emerge in the trade business. However, be wary of unevenness in various matters during the year of destiny. As a result, to break the bad luck and attract the auspicious stars, you should strengthen your prestige by practicing dharma, making merit, and donating to the underprivileged. Any work activities this year should not be underestimated, and they should always be done with care and consideration. But because a bad star will invade the house of fate during the year. The effects of "Dawn Sing" (Danger Planet), "Kuang Sor" (Shackle Star), and "Nine Satellite" (Blue Dog) on health, sickness, accidents, and property loss are direct. As a result, this year is not suitable for investing in projects with high risk or a lack of expertise because you are likely to incur losses due to unforeseen circumstances. As a result, when investing or forming joint ventures this year, exercise extreme caution and be wary of accounting fraud. Be cautious of a lack of working capital liquidity. Be wary of being duped by others who use forged documents in various transactions. Furthermore, be cautious that you may sustain an injury, be hurt, or become ill as a result of a disease that threatens to cause marital conflict. You must be aware that expressing your frustration with others will cause those around you to flee. This year should begin with focusing on your physical health. Take care of your mental health, have strength, and feel at ease, when you are not stressed, you can control your emotions, you should not make enemies, you should not make others hate you, and you should try to avoid hurling your bad temper at others.

Career and Business

Even this year, the direction of your trading business will be monsoon, but amid the difficulties, you will find helpers to keep your work and business on track. However, you should find an heir to take over the work. Even if you have a hundred stamina to work today, looking for an agent is not critical, but finding one early will allow you to transfer the job. Especially the months in which the work will change in a better direction, such as the 2nd month of China (6 Mar. – 4 Apr.), the 6th month of China (7 Jul. – 7 Aug.), the 8th month of China (8 Sep. – 7 Oct.) and 9th month of China (8 Oct. – 6 Nov.) Now looking for an heir to manage investments both inside and outside the company. A satisfactory return and expected outcomes are anticipated. But be careful during the months that your work will encounter problems such as the 1st month of China (4 Feb. - 5 Mar.), the 4th month of China (6 May - 5 Jun.), the 7th month of China. (8 Aug. – 7 Sep.) , and the 10th month of China (7 Nov. – 6 Dec). Investing during that period has the potential to be deceptive. Furthermore, those who do not wish well to persuade them to invest more may lose any contract documents related to work. Don't be taken in by flattery without first verifying the facts; it's the source of the loss and loss.

Financial

The financial fortunes of this year are mixed. Be wary of unforeseen current expenditures that will drain money from the system, and avoid being greedy for small sums that will cause them to waste large sums of money. Unnecessary expenses should be saved as a reserve. And can be used in an emergency, as well as allocate the appropriate investment. Because they have the right to be hurt if they enter the market in the wrong way at the wrong time. Especially during the months when your finances are down, such as the 1st month of China (4 Feb. – 5 Mar.), the 4th month of China (6 May – 5 Jun), the 7th month of China (8 Aug. – 7 Sep) and the 10th month of China (7 Nov. – 6 Dec.). Please do not allow others to borrow money or guarantee to anyone during this time. Do not gamble, do not invest in risky and illegal businesses, join ventures with others, or invest in securities during such times to avoid damage.

For the month that your finances will flow smoothly, including 2nd month of China (6 Mar. – 4 Apr.), the 6th month of China (7 Jul. – 7 Aug.), the 8th month of China (8 Sep. – 7 Oct.), and the 9th month of China (8 Oct. – 6 Nov.).

Family
However, there will be an auspicious event in the house this year. There will be good things coming your way, but you should be wary of the influence of the harassing stars, which may cause envy among those you know and pose a danger to those in your home. Especially the months that were not smooth and chaotic were the 1st month of China (4 Feb. – 5 Mar.), the 4th

month of China (6 May – 5 Jun.), the 7th month of China (8 Aug. – 7 Sep) and the 10th month of China (7 Nov. – 6 Dec.) where you must exercise extreme caution in a variety of situations Should not interfere in the internal affairs or litigation problems of relatives; avoid accidents at home and medical expenses for close relatives. Be wary of people in the house being duped into becoming involved in a lawsuit that disrupts the peace. Also, be wary of lost valuables and be prepared to grieve for elderly relatives.

Love
This year, the beginning and end of the year went smoothly, but there will be problems with disputes in the middle of the year. You and your spouse will have feuds and be estranged. Children will deceive them, so be careful not to fall for them. As a result, to lessen the possibility of misunderstanding between you and your lover. You must maintain your equilibrium. Always think before you act, and everything will pass. Furthermore, be wary of mood swings from your golden years, which can make you irritable and thus easily provoke

arguments. Especially during the following months, i.e. 1st month of China (4 Feb. – 5 Mar.), 4th month of China (6 May – 5 Jun.), 7th month of China (8 Aug. – 7 Sep.), and 10th month of China (7 Nov. – 6 Dec.) Wherever you go to parties, be cautious of the big house misunderstanding. You should avoid interfering in other people's family matters. Take care not to let your children in front of you. It is best not to meddle in the affairs of children. Avoid going to places of entertainment that may make you sick as a bonus.

Health

Your health is suffering as a result of the unlucky stars' influence. So be cautious, as a silent disease emerges to make you sick. You should make time to rest. Trying to avoid all vices, such as smoking, drinking, and so on, because they are all bad for your health. You should also be aware of abnormal blood pressure. Shortness of breath, heart disease and symptoms of blood supply to the brain will not result in fainting. So getting enough sleep is beneficial. Make time to exercise and see a doctor as soon as possible. If you suspect something is wrong, Especially during the months that you should pay special attention to health care, such as the 1st month of China (4 Feb. - 5 Mar.), the 4th month of China (6 May - 5 Jun), the 7th month of China (8 Aug. - 7 Sep) and the 10th month of China (7 Nov. - 6 Dec.), where the fate should be strict on food hygiene, sugar, saltiness, and avoiding high-fat foods. Be wary of new and old illnesses that beset and request them, and be extra cautious about accidents at work and on the road.

Year of the PIG (Gold) | (1971)
" The Pig is in the coop." is a person born in the year of the PIG at the age of 52 years (1971)

Overview
Because the planet orbiting his destiny house this year is the "Star," Lord Destiny is around this age.

"Sao Kuang" (Dow Chains) On the bright side, this year is another auspicious year in which your efforts will not be in vain. Job responsibilities will increase. Trades will grow in popularity. Outside investments, such as buying and selling shares, have a good direction, and you will have the opportunity to buy at the right price at the right time and sell at a satisfactory price, or you will receive a satisfactory dividend if you buy and keep. However, during the year, a bad start to visits, namely, "Dao Guang Sao" (star chain) and "Nine satellite" (Blue Dog star), will have a significant impact on negligent investment, and lack of caution will find numbers. Negative, characterized by either economic volatility or uncontrollable market dynamics. It will be a major source of your financial insecurity. You should also avoid arguing with other people in the house. Both will attract bullies and cannot afford to ignore health issues. Accidental illnesses and injuries can occur both at work and while traveling. As a result, exercise caution for your safety.

Career and Business

The work for this year is for government officials or government officials. This year, there will be an opportunity to adjust the position for a better job, but those who work for a salary should be wary of subordinates who cause trouble. Those who conduct business should continue to visit their customers. The account release must be cautious not to focus solely on sales growth. Especially during the months when your work will encounter chaos and congestion, such as the 1st month of China (4 Feb. – 5 Mar.), the 4th month of China (6 May – 5 Jun)., the 7th month of China (8 Aug. – 7 Sep.) and 10th month of China (7 Nov. – 6 Dec.) Be cautious of bad accounts receivable. Make no decisions that are simply tempered or provoked by defiance. Before taking action, every work activity should be viewed and carefully examined. Furthermore, you should be aware of personnel management issues, what to do, not be impatient, make decisions, and exercise caution in controlling your emotions. Try not to flaunt your displeasure. Regardless of whether one is challenged or ridiculed, one must try to remain calm. and demonstrate your purity.

For the months in which your work, including trade, has a better direction, namely, the 2nd month of China (6 Mar. - 4 Apr.), the 6th month of China (7 Jul. - 7 Aug.)., the 8th month of China (8 Sep. – 7 Oct.) and the 9th month in China (8 Oct. – 6 Nov.).

Financial

Although the cash flow from salary or sales will be substantial this year. Furthermore, money from special events and the floating fortune will contribute significantly. However, due to the villain's influence, there is frequently a reason to lose a large sum of money unexpectedly. Be especially careful during the following months: 1st month of China (4 Feb. – 5 Mar.), the 4th month of China (6 May. – 5 Jun.), 7th month of China (8 Aug. – 7 Sep), and the 10th month of China (7 Nov. – 6 Dec.) that close relatives are not permitted to borrow money or accept guarantees. Do not engage in gambling. Do not engage in any illegal business. Do not be overly greedy, and be wary of wealth loss caused by a minor or a follower. Unnecessary expenses should be cut. Always strive to learn more to stay current with the situation and open up more revenue channels.

As for the months in which your finances will flow smoothly, they are the 2nd month of China (6 Mar. – 4 Apr.), 6th month of China (7 Jul. – 7 Aug.), 8th month of China (8 Sep. – 7 Oct.) and the 9th month of China (8 Oct. – 6 Nov.).

Family

Because of the influence of evil stars, this year's family has lost their peace. The trick may be solved by fate by purchasing items at the price he prefers at the start of the year. Considered a solution to property loss and should be cautious of people in the house arguing with neighbors until it becomes resentment that looks to account, causing a lack of peace on both sides. Especially during the months when families will encounter conflicts, such as the 1st month of China (4 Feb. – 5 Mar.), the 4th month of China (6 May – 5 Jun), the 7th month of China (8 Aug - 7 Sep) and the 10th month of China (7 Nov - 6 Dec) to be more cautious, especially when it comes to family members' illnesses and the use of other people's tools Injuries will occur in the home as a result of accidents. Be wary of bringing legal action against others. As a result, you are not permitted to intervene if your friends are disagreeing this year. Avoid getting involved in a lawsuit and getting into trouble. You may also be hated and seek vengeance, as well as be on the lookout for valuables that have been damaged or stolen.

Love

This year's love of your destiny is not going to be easy; it will be easy to get caught up in the storm. You must be cautious not to let it explode too easily. Otherwise, the path will only lead to failure. Especially during the months when your love is fragile and will be prone to problems such as the 1st month of China (4 Feb. – 5 Mar.), the 4th month of China (6 May. – 5 Jun.). , the 7th month of China (8 Aug. – 7 Sep.), and the 10th month of China (7 Nov. – 6 Dec.), Avoid interfering with other people's family problems. Be wary of the third party who will intrude and cause misunderstandings. Furthermore, avoid roaming in entertainment venues to avoid getting sick.

Health

The influence of the orbiting villain directly focusing on the health base weakened this year's destiny's health. You may be unaware of the dangers of injury, bleeding from objects, sharp objects, and accidents and illnesses. Especially during the month when health issues, such as the 1st month of China (4 Feb. – 5 Mar.), the 4th month of China (6 May. – 5 Jun.), the 7th month of China (8 Aug. - 7 Sep), and the 10th month of China (7 Nov. - 6 Dec.) Be wary of fainting and fainting spells. Do not drive or operate machinery if you have consumed alcohol or are suffering from a hangover.

Year of the PIG (Water) | (1983)

" The Pig is in the forest." is a person born in the year of the PIG at the age of 40 years (1983)

Overview

For this age's destiny Because the planet that orbits your destiny this year is the "snare star" (danger planet), now is a good time to find a patron for your career and progress. Trades will find new opportunities. As a result, the most important aspect of this year's behavior is human relations skills. There should be a good working relationship between the upper and lower levels. Maintain friendships and business relationships at all times. You should also motivate yourself by constantly seeking knowledge to improve your ability to be flexible and adapt to changing circumstances. Goals and achievements will not be far behind. However, the year in the destiny house was plagued by a swarm of evil stars in orbit. This group of stars will hurt you and your family. Accidents, arguments, and legal issues should all be avoided. You must not be careless in your life or when driving. Arguments should also avoid long responses. Litigation should be resolved by following the law, being humble, and being willing to compromise. Having good interpersonal skills, as well as being diligent and patient, will provide you with a bright future in which to achieve your goals. Another thing to keep in mind this year is that making friends must be done with caution. If you put too much faith in your friends, you may end up coming to your heart's content.

Career and Business

Destiny's trade was not at its peak at this time, but it was also not at its lowest. Because if you run into problems this year, you will be able to find a sponsor to assist you. have the opportunity to receive assistance from adults and colleagues As a result, I ask you to work hard, and you will undoubtedly produce results in the eyes of your boss. Sales will be good or bad if you run your own business or trade this year. It also depends on having a good relationship with the people with whom you must maintain constant contact. As a result, it can increase sales. Especially during the months when your work and trade will change in a better direction, such as the 2nd month of China (6 Mar. – 4 Apr.), the 6th month of China (7 Jul. – 7 Aug.) the 8th month of China (8 Sep. – 7 Oct.) and the 9th month of China (8 Oct. – 6 Nov.). However, you should be careful during the months that your work will suffer. Congestion problems are: 1st month of China (4 Feb. – 5 Mar.), 4th month of China (6 May – 5

Jun.), 7th month of China (8 Aug. – 7 Sep.) and the 10th month of China (7 Nov. – 6 Dec.) During this period, the contract of employment or employment, you should carefully review the terms of the contract before making a decision. Furthermore, should not invest in new things or increase investment, and should be wary of the minority that causes trouble.

Financial

During this period, the contract of employment or employment, you should carefully review the terms of the contract before making a decision. Furthermore, should not invest in new things or increase investment, and should be wary of the minority that causes trouble: 2nd month of China (6 Mar. – 4 Apr.) 6th month of China (7 Jul. – 7 Aug.), 8th month of China (8 Sep. – 7 Oct.) and 9th month of China (8 Oct. – 6 Nov.), However, unexpected expenses will appear to catch up with income. There will be some left if you know how to save and save. However, if you are careless, you have the right to remove the dry face. Especially during the following months, i.e., 1st month of China (4 Feb. – 5 Mar.), 4th month of China (6 May – 5

Jun.), 7th month of China (8 Aug. – 7 Sep.), and 10th month of China (7 Nov. – 6 Dec.) that makes lending and receiving guarantees illegal. Do not engage in gambling. Do not invest in companies that violate the law. Should be careful with the liquid in the bag. Otherwise, a financial crisis could occur.

Family

The family horoscope for this year is a criterion for finding auspiciousness within the evil hidden. Even if auspicious stars are promoted, bad stars are discovered to be blocking it, so destiny should be cautious. Specifically, the people in the house's health and safety issues, as well as conflicts and mourning for senior relatives. Especially during the months in which your family will have troubles, such as the 1st month of China (4 Feb. – 5 Mar.), the 4th month of China (6 May. – 5 Jun.), 7th month of China (8 Aug. – 7 Sep.) and 10th month of China (7 Nov. – 6 Dec.) where you need to increase home security and safety precautions, such as roofs, ceilings, and appliances Power, as well as other high-altitude fixtures If something breaks, it should be replaced or repaired so that it can be used again. Reduce the factors that cause disagreements among family members. Also, be wary of valuables that have been damaged or stolen. Furthermore, they should be able to analyze and distinguish between friends who are friends with whom they conceal some peculiarities to be safe. Furthermore, you should avoid becoming involved in internal matters or disputes arising from a friend's lawsuit.

Love

Because of the power of the Huai (the power of charm, magic) combined with the demon star "Kuang Sor" (the chain star) that orbits, this year's love threatens to focus on your love, leaving you with a lack of stability in mind, often skeptical, and frequently appearing as a third hand waiting to snore and have opinions in the way. Same as before, no promotion, nothing, so it appears to be a problem. You should be cautious during the months when your love is quite fragile and conflicts are likely such as the 1st month of China (4 Feb. - 5 Mar.), the 4th month of China (6 May - 5 Jun.), 7th month of China (8 Aug. - 7 Sep.) and 10th month of China (7 Nov. - 6 Dec.) Be careful not to interfere with other people's families. and be careful of swear words that will affect your spouse's heart. Avoid going to entertainment places and sources of malice.

Health

The health situation this year is moderate; there will be some sickness, but the cure is not serious. However, the power of the deceased Huai was threatened by fate. Causing the destiny to have diseases related to love and harassment "Dao Huai Yim" (Blood Sharp Star), which will affect the danger of injury, hemorrhage, and other annoying illnesses come to mind. By the month that you have to take care of your health closely, such as the 1st month of China (4 Feb. – 5 Mar.), the 4th month of China (6 May. – 5 Jun.), and the 7th month of China. (8 Aug. – 7 Sep.) and 10th month of China (7 Nov. – 6 Dec.).

Year of the PIG (Wood) | (1995)

" The Pig live the Temple" is a person born in the year of the PIG at the age of 28 years (1995)

Overview

This year, the planet orbiting your zodiac sign is the "shackle star," so every activity should be reflected to act. The work should be communicated to understand the work that is produced and to avoid errors. When it comes to education, you have the option of studying both at home and abroad. If the request for a scholarship to study further has a reasonable contract, you should not pass it up. Knowing humility is a good thing to learn from your seniors if you work. You must both diligently learn to develop yourself to keep up with ever-changing situations and know how to be flexible and adapt to pave the way for a bright future. There is a good chance of getting a job in the government or starting your own business. However, accidents will occur due to the shackles of evil stars and dangerous planets in the zodiac. Unexpected current expenditures result in a lack of liquidity. This year, you should carefully plan your spending because if you enjoy spending, you may suffer. If you have to flee to uninformed debt, it will make it more difficult to start a new job, enter shares, or invest in various fields. This year, there is a high likelihood of being duped. Be cautious or you may suffer a loss.

Career and Business

If your destiny chooses to continue your studies this year, then this is a good opportunity for you, so persisting in your studies will encourage you to have a bright future. Always learn and develop yourself if you choose to work or run your own business. Understand how to take a step back and listen. Don't be biased; it will help you later in the process. You should cultivate positive relationships with both your supervisors and your coworkers. It will lead to a successful career. During the month in which your work or trading business will experience difficulties, such as the 1st month of China (4 Feb. – 5 Mar.), the 4th month of China (6 May. – 5 Jun.), 7th month of China (8 Aug. – 7 Sep.) and 10th month of China (7 Nov. – 6 Dec.), Work cannot be rushed; mistakes may occur. Signing any contracts During this time, you should double-check everything to ensure there are no problems later. Furthermore, you should not reinvest or increase your investment because you have the right to be misled.

For the month that your work and trade will have a bright direction, namely, the 2nd month of China (6 Mar. - 4 Apr.), the 6th month of China (7 Jul. - 7 Aug.), the 8th month of China (8 Sep. – 7 Oct.) and 9th month of China (8 Oct. – 6 Nov.).

Financial

The fortune's financial fortunes rise and fall. Even this year, the floating fortune will provide enough funds, but if you are extremely greedy, you have the right to be pessimistic. As a result, financial planning is critical. You should also take care of the liquidity of your working capital to avoid any business disruptions. You should also avoid engaging in any illegal activity. Otherwise, you will become entangled in a web of trouble. Especially during the months when the financial stumble, such as the

1st month of China (4 Feb. – 5 Mar.), the 4th month of China (6 May. – 5 Jun.), the 7th month of China (8 Aug. – 7 Sep) and the 10th month of China (7 Nov – 6 Dec.), which makes borrowing money or receiving guarantees illegal. You should avoid gambling and gambling, and you should be wary of theft. They must also be cautious of unexpected large expenditures that will result in a lack of liquidity. For the month in which your finances are in order, include 2nd month of China (6 Mar. – 4 Apr.), 6th month of China (7 Jul. – 7 Aug.), the 8th month of China (8 Sep – 7 Oct.), and the 9th month of China (8 Oct. – 6 Nov.).

Family

This year will have both good and bad events in your family. The good news is that you will find patrons willing to assist you. The worst part will be the villain's aftermath, which will cause accidents and have an impact on the health and safety of the elderly and family members. You may be in mourning for your elderly relatives, especially during the months when the family is in turmoil. Including the 1st month of China (4 Feb. - 5 Mar.), the 4th month of China (6 May.

- 5 Jun.). , 7th month of China (8 Aug. – 7 Sep.) and 10th month of China (7 Nov. – 6 Dec.) Be wary of squabbles with housemates. Also, be wary of valuables that have been misplaced or stolen.

This year's relatives and friends are in good health. You will find good friends to give you work advice in the overview. Make suggestions for ways to make a living. Help with something you're not very good at. However, be cautious because some of your ungrateful friends are dishonest, putting your bad deeds to shame.

Love
The love is sweet at the start of the first six months, and the vegetable broth is still sweet, but by the middle of the year, into the six months after you see anything, you are completely offended. Even if you find a temporary love, a stronger charm than this, you must exercise restraint. Make use of your awareness. Distinguish the love of the self-sufficient individual. Especially during the month that your love will have problems, and quarrels easily, such as the 1st month of China

(4 Feb. – 5 Mar.), the 4th month of China (6 May – 5 Jun.), the 7th month of China. (8 Aug. – 7 Sep.) and 10th month of China (7 Nov. – 6 Dec.) should use caution when speaking and avoid trains on time You shouldn't give it a chance if you don't have a heart. Because it will lead to misunderstandings and arguments. Also, avoid going to places of entertainment that may spread disease.

Health

This year's health horoscope for this age group is not favorable, so be wary of the risk of bleeding from an accident. Especially during the months when you should pay close attention to your health, such as the 1st month of China (4 Feb. - 5 Mar.), the 4th month of China (6 May. - 5 Jun.). In the 7th month of China (8 Aug. – 7 Sep.) and the 10th month of China (7 Nov. – 6 Dec.), Use extra caution when working with machinery or metal equipment. Driving a vehicle, driving a car, driving on the road, don't be careless, and practice good drinking and eating hygiene. Avoid intoxicants, alcohol, and cigarettes, which will harm your health.

Chinese Astrology Horoscope for Each Month

Month 12 in the Tiger Year (6 Jan 23 - 3 Feb 23)

Starting this month, your destiny that was born in the Year of the Pig has moved to find the line of destruction with a group of evil stars orbiting to harass the important thing that you should be cautious of. Pretending to wait for the moment when you will again miss the big bang. As a result, if you are thinking about doing any work or planning on any matter, you must be more cautious in every situation. and always have a backup plan in place in case of unexpected changes.

What you should do this month is to do good while not standing out as a threat, whether in speech, posture, gestures, or overall interpersonal skills. Both should be known for their humility. It is preferable to be gentle than to save you from adversity. You should also double-check the accounting system and manage working capital more closely. Anything that is overpowered, don't be too stubborn, will make it more difficult to move the liquidity forward.

Monsoons disrupt work, including business, during this period. Conflicts within the agency should be avoided. Be wary of unanticipated interference that could jeopardize your main work. However, you should do your best to carry out your responsibilities while remaining impartial and fair to those under your supervision. Also, during this time, be careful not to sign any contract documents related to the trade that could lead to deception or disadvantage.

Lose the property because the horoscope of this salary falls on the seat. As a result, spending should be prudent. You should not gamble or be greedy.

The family is moderate; they should spend more time together.

The love horoscope is favorable; find the opposite sex appealing, and love is found. However, going to an entertainment venue to find temporary love may result in a reactive disease.

Relatives are not ideal. As a result, don't lend money because you might not get it back. Nothing should be invested as an investment. Also, avoid interfering with gambling.

The state of health was moderate. You should continue to exercise and eat a healthy diet.

Support Days: 1 Jan., 5 Jan., 9 Jan., 13 Jan., 17 Jan., 21 Jan., 25 Jan., 29 Jan.
Lucky Days: 8 Jan., 20 Jan.
Misfortune Days: 11 Jan., 23 Jan.
Bad Days: 2 Jan., 14 Jan., 26 Jan.

Month 1 in the Rabbit Year (4 Feb 23 - 5 Mar 23)
This month's horoscope predicts a major storm that will have an impact on work and management. Those of you who work regularly will face obstacles such as conflicts and chaos of people, which will cause headaches. Those who conduct business will encounter adversaries who intercept and block. To increase market share and customer base, all strategies must be implemented.

Be wary of minors in the workplace who may cause problems for you to follow. Furthermore, contract negotiations and agreements must be detailed and prudent. Work cannot be impatient because it can easily lead to mistakes.

Starting a new job, investing, or forming a joint venture this month is not a good time.

This month, here's what you should do. Reduce conflict by managing human resources. Also, exercise caution. Don't be a source of contention. Also, avoid using emotions at work. They will be able to overcome various obstacles if the tasks assigned to them are clearly understood before taking action.

This salary horoscope collides with the monsoon. As a result, you should not allow anyone to borrow money or accept guarantees. Do not take chances with your luck. You should save money, look for ways to increase your income, and maintain the liquidity of your working capital.

The family is peaceful, but watch out for gastritis, intestinal disease, and food poisoning. Accidents can happen at home or while traveling, and they can cause injury.

Do not listen to incitement to gossip when you are in love. Avoid interfering in other people's families and avoid arguments. Avoid going to entertainment venues because you may become ill as a result.

During this time, be wary of relatives and friends who are two-faced, acting behind your back and causing you harm.

Support Days: 2 Feb., 6 Feb., 10 Feb., 14 Feb., 18 Feb., 22 Feb., 26 Feb.
Lucky Days: 1 Feb., 13 Feb., 25 Feb.
Misfortune Days: 4 Feb., 16 Feb., 28 Feb.
Bad Days: 7 Feb., 19 Feb.

Month 2 in the Rabbit Year (6 Mar 23 - 5 Apr 23)
This month, your destiny has shifted to meet the alliance, and it is supported by the shining auspicious stars. Many stuck issues can be encouraged to continue working smoothly. You will have the opportunity to produce results that will help you progress in your job duties. The trading industry will have a good chance of making money.

You should be more diligent in your work this month because you can do a lot, create a lot of work, expand sales, increase income, and drive various projects. that you intended to become concrete quickly and without stumbling blocks

This salary horoscope is favorable; there are cash inflows in both directions, directly from the regular salary. Money from special events, as well as money from fortune, has poured in. However, you must also understand how to save money for the month when your finances are tight.

In terms of the fate of a peaceful family, auspicious power visits you. You meet the criteria for receiving good news about the success of the people in the house.

There are criteria for organizing any auspicious event within the family, there may be adding new members, or you may have the opportunity to move into a new home.

The mild climate contributes to good health, even with minor illnesses. However, you cannot be careless about accidents while traveling both near and far this month.

In terms of sweet and seductive love, the opposite sex is more interested in getting closer this month.

Your family and friends will be very supportive.

This period will yield good returns on investments in a variety of fields.

Support Days: 2 Mar, 6 Mar., 10 Mar., 14 Mar., 18 Mar., 22 Mar., 26 Mar., 30 Mar.
Lucky Days: 9 Mar, 21 Mar.
Misfortune Days: 12 Mar, 24 Mar.
Bad Days: 3 Mar, 15 Mar., 27 Mar.

Month 3 in the Rabbit Year (6 Apr 23 - 5 May 23) Although your destiny is improving this month, the major issues that are bothering you have not faded. That is quite volatile when combined with your mind. Only agitation and anxiety prevent problems from being seen, causing them to miss out on good opportunities.

This month, you should investigate yourself, discovering your weaknesses and strengths. what is the possibility Should look for ways to improve strengths and opportunities to thrive in the future. Most importantly, you must be decisive and act quickly to resolve any existing issues. Because the horoscope contains patrons, your mind is still hesitant. As a result, in terms of investment work, if you think carefully and thoroughly, you can take action.

Gambling may not be the main concern in this salary horoscope, middle income. It's better to play for fun with a limited amount of money than to be too greedy until your fortune is gone. Furthermore, do not underestimate. Revenue must be divided into parts for saving and investing.

The time has come to plan for major projects, according to the business horoscope. If you are in business, it is time to plan your purchase budget to reopen the market and expand new channels. You should prepare to gather resources and manpower.

This month has been peaceful for the family. There is nothing to be concerned about.

However, in good health, even if you have an old disease, you will feel better. However, it should be treated on an ongoing basis because it may relapse into a larger problem. You should always maintain a good living and eating hygiene.

Love horoscope is the honeymoon period for singles, and the relationship is going swimmingly. A second or third honeymoon vacation is ideal for those with small families.

You will receive assistance from family members and friends.

Support Days: 3 Apr., 7 Apr., 11 Apr., 15 Apr., 19 Apr., 23 Apr., 27 Apr.
Lucky Days: 2 Apr., 14 Apr., 26 Apr.
Misfortune Days: 5 Apr., 17 Apr., 29 Apr.
Bad Days: 8 Apr., 20 Apr.

Month 4 in the Rabbit Year (6 May 23 - 5 Jun 23)
This month, the path of your life took you closer to the end. As a result, the story of obstacles merged with both chaos and chaos. If not properly managed, the good relationship that has been established may be lost.

This month, here's what you should do. Full-strength performance of his assigned duties. Avoids having disagreements with those around you. It's known as putting yourself first. So gradually go out and help and advise others. In addition, when it comes to conflicts, you must remain neutral. Make it clear that you are not siding with either party. and should always maintain a humble and respectful demeanor. If there is a problem at work, fix it as soon as possible. Do not wait so long that it becomes difficult to heal. Both should be cautious of accidents while at work and on the road.

This salary horoscope is not favorable. Be wary of unforeseen current expenditures and bad debts if you have a low income and a high expenditure. Do not gamble or invest in illegal enterprises. because they may face the dangers of incarceration

Workplace personnel management that causes conflicts should be avoided. Be wary of accounting fraud and workplace errors.

Investing and stock trading should be avoided during this time.

Concerning the family, care must be taken to ensure the safety of those in the home. Be wary of the members' arguments as well. and thieves break in and steal small items

This month is favorable for health, but be cautious of injury from unexpected accidents. Disaster may result from a quarrel, or you may be held jointly liable in a friend's lawsuit.

In terms of love, if you get stuck, your lover will assist you. And now is an excellent time for singles to open their hearts to love.

However, relatives and friends may have to keep their distance during this time because it will cause problems.

Support Days: 1 May., 5 May., 9 May., 13 May., 17 May., 21 May., 25 May., 29 May
Lucky Days: 8 May., 20 May.
Misfortune Days: 11 May., 23 May.

Month 5 in the Rabbit Year (6 Jun 23 - 6 Jul 23)
This month, your destiny, born in the Year of the Pig, moves to meet the stars that help support you. The road of life soared once more. This is yet another favorable time for expansion plans. No need to think twice about expanding the planned channel; just do it. There are also patrons to assist and support. As a result, be determined and diligent to pursue your goals to the fullest; do not let this opportunity pass you by. This month, it is critical that you get up early and work harder than anyone else. Otherwise, competitors may seize the opportunity and money available.

This salary horoscope is abundant in earnings from sales, earnings, and extra money from part-time work. However, fortune floats back to the dark side. As a result, avoid any risky investments and the risk of being hurt. This month should be free of alcohol.

In terms of work, find a way to progress and run a successful business. To succeed, however, you must be filled with both courage and diligence.

The family horoscope in the house is harmonious, there is auspicious power, and there will be happy news about success or an auspicious event to attend.

In terms of love, this month is sweet and happy. However, you must continue to pay attention to keep adding sweetness to your marriage and not neglect the time you should spend with your family. However, the emphasis should be on appropriately allocating time to work and love. For the destiny who is still unmarried If the person you love is determined to marry, I urge you to speak up and negotiate to make it happen. Otherwise, you risk being severed by a good hand and losing your loved one.
Nothing to be concerned about in terms of health.

However, relatives and friends must exercise caution because some friends are on the verge of being stabbed in the back.

Both are unsuitable for starting a new job, joining a joint venture, or investing because bad intentions will be present to deceive and cause damage and trouble.

Support Days: 2 Jun., 6 Jun., 10 Jun., 14 Jun., 18 Jun., 22 Jun., 26 Jun., 30 Jun.
Lucky Days: 1 Jun., 13 Jun., 25 Jun.
Misfortune Days: 4 Jun., 16 Jun., 28 Jun.
Bad Days: 7 Jun., 19 Jun.

Month 6 in the Rabbit Year (7 Jul 23 - 7 Aug 23)
Your fate criteria, Even with the auspicious stars shining brightly, this month brings about many positive changes. However, trade is still hampered as a result of the monsoon. There are also conflicts between individuals within the organization that cannot be resolved for them to be reconciled. As a result, this month you should remember that creating a positive work

environment begins with your patience. Use sincerity of forgiveness to withstand various frictions. It will aid in the resolution of conflicts.

This salary horoscope is a shambles. You will incur unanticipated costs. Don't gamble, try your luck, and don't be greedy. because it will result in more harm

Be wary of problems with customers or people with whom you frequently interact this month. It should be addressed so that it does not become a problem in the future.

As medicine and counselors, family destiny will find helpers. Things that are grieving and suffering will improve.
Lovers should be patient because love is not always easy. Don't rely solely on your emotions or self-centeredness. If your destiny is single, keep looking for a close time.

To maintain good health, avoid air allergies, allergies, liver disease, gastritis, intestinal disease, and excessive alcohol consumption. Avoid mishaps at work and on the road.

It is moderate in terms of relatives and friends, not good, not bad.

If you are serious about investing, you should seek the advice of an experienced adult. Otherwise, problems will arise in the future.

Support Days: 4 Jul., 8 Jul., 12 Jul., 16 Jul., 20 Jul., 24 Jul., 28 Jul.
Lucky Days: 7 Jul., 19 Jul., 31 Jul.
Misfortune Days: 10 Jul., 22 Jul.
Bad Days: 1 Jul., 13 Jul., 25 Jul.

Month 7 in the Rabbit Year (8 Aug 23 - 7 Sep 23)
This month, your destiny has shifted to find a line of punishment. As a result, the upward trajectory of destiny lowered the level. As a result, work and business faced new challenges and had to deal with daily concerns about minors or dependents causing damage. Keep an eye out for fraudulent misappropriation of

accounting or contract documents. You must be cautious during this time to avoid being duped into a disadvantage. As a result, before engaging in any activity, you should examine it thoroughly. In terms of management, interpersonal conflicts must be handled with extreme caution. The most important thing to remember at this time is to be mindful and not overstress yourself.

You should do some important things during this time. Don't rush to present yourself when you find a story. This draw may find favor, as well as the right to suffer injuries on behalf of others. In addition, this month, spend time with friends whose faces you don't recognize. Be cautious with your sweet mouth, but keep the knife hidden behind your back.

This salary's horoscopes fall on the seat and lose money. There will be unimaginable emergency costs. When income is low and expenses are high, it should be more cost-effective. Gambling on this month's luck should be avoided. and forbids lending or investing in illegal enterprises. Don't be too greedy to expect others' fortunes. Also, be wary of bad debts from customers with outstanding accounts that will result in bad debts.

There are evil stars in chains and dangerous planets to focus on for the family. As a result, be mindful of the safety and health of those in your home. and beware of mourning for elderly relatives to avoid losing or stealing valuables

There is room for debate when it comes to love and destiny. As a result, one should avoid going to entertainment venues or interfering with the lives of others, and one should take care to have a third hand inserted in the middle.

At this time, the most important health concern is insomnia. Also, be cautious of injury from accidents while working or driving.

It is not a good time for relatives and friends, investments, or work.

Support Days: 1 Aug., 5 Aug., 9 Aug., 13 Aug., 17 Aug., 21 Aug., 25 Aug., 29 Aug.
Lucky Days: 12 Aug., 24 Aug.
Misfortune Days: 3 Aug., 15 Aug., 27 Aug.
Bad Days: 9 Aug., 21 Aug.

Month 8 in the Rabbit Year (8 Sep 23 - 7 Oct 23)
Since last month's work and business activities met with success, this month's horoscope continues to prosper. A bird caught in the wind on the top, for example, can fly and glide for long distances. So, remember to make good connections at both the top and bottom this month, because big tasks are not meant to be completed alone. All parties must pitch in to help.

This salary is good, very diligent, and will bring in a lot of money, according to the horoscope. Income is coming in from a variety of sources. Salary income and sales There will also be an opportunity to receive additional funds from the fortune. Some people in need of funds may begin collecting this month. Those seeking additional income may enroll in vocational courses to open doors for themselves. You will have a verbal charm this month. As a result, you should cultivate positive relationships with your customers or those with whom you must interact. It will aid in the advancement of your work.

Commercial work will be difficult at this time because communication should not be rushed to judge, but should instead focus on clearly communicating. Furthermore, the conflict lingers in the shadows. You must be courageous enough to make decisions that are unresolved to the least damaging conclusion. Because if it drags on for too long, nothing will improve and it will be worse off than before.

This month's family horoscope predicts that there will be disagreements in the home. including those on the inside arguing with strangers Avoid it by staying out of other people's business.

A good love horoscope indicates the best time for auspicious events, such as marriage proposals or weddings.

Your health is good, but don't forget to get some exercise.

On the side of good friends, but watch out for words that may inadvertently hurt others.

You can choose to invest this month if you want to start a new job, join a joint venture, or invest in various fields.

Support Days: 2 Sep, 6 Sep., 10 Sep, 14 Sep, 18 Sep., 22 Sep., 26 Sep., 30 Sep.
Lucky Days: 5 Sep, 17 Sep., 29 Sep.
Misfortune Days: 8 Sep, 20 Sep.
Bad Days: 11 Sep, 23 Sep.

Month 9 in the Rabbit Year (8 Oct 23 - 6 Nov 23)
This month, your destiny shifts into the alliance line. There is also an auspicious star that shines with auspicious energy, granting patronage to those who visit and assist in dispelling all unlucky powers. As a result, if the opportunity arises, you should continue to make merits and merits to help relieve the suffering from heavy to light.

When the opportunity presents itself, you should do something important. You should proceed with caution to carry out the plans that have been made. This opportunity will yield positive results. Furthermore, honesty should be used to defeat rivals. and make those you must interact with see your genuine concern for others.

Good fortune, direct finance, and good inflows mean that liquidity remains bright. However, you must be careful not to overburden your heart. You should only spend when necessary; otherwise, you will get into trouble later. Furthermore, the fortune of fortune is small.

So, don't be greedy when it comes to knowing enough.

In terms of your work, you will continue to progress. This could be because the problem was resolved and assistance was found to assist in resolving the issue.

The family horoscope is typical. However, you must exercise caution when it comes to joy. This time will be merely a castle in the air, leaving you disappointed.

Love is silky. Lovers will spoil each other All I ask is that you not be sweet in the wrong way. Importantly, flowers along the road should not be plucked because there may be dangers.

This month is going well for family and friends. Relatives who were once estranged will reconnect, understand each other, and love and be more generous to one another.

This month will be favorable for a variety of investments.

Your health, despite a few minor illnesses. To build immunity, eat nutritious foods and exercise regularly.

Support Days: 4 Oct., 8 Oct., 12 Oct., 16 Oct., 20 Oct., 24 Oct., 28 Oct.
Lucky Days: 11 Oct., 23 Oct.
Misfortune Days: 2 Oct., 14 Oct., 26 Oct.
Bad Days: 5 Oct., 17 Oct., 29 Oct.

Month 10 in the Rabbit Year (7 Nov 23 - 6 Dec 23)
Because the road of life this month moves to meet the evil constellation, your destiny will go downhill, causing obstacles in the trade. There are frequent competitors to compete and cut the front. Furthermore, the influence of the stars frequently causes accidents or unforeseen events, including health issues. As a result, you must exercise greater caution and remain calm during all activities. Do not be overly greedy or greedy, as this may result in property damage or loss.

The main things you should do this month are: Should adhere to the principle of savings and take care of liquidity and working capital in the business to be careful of leaks. If you find a story, don't leave the page. Both be careful to drink and eat. Be careful when the liquor gets into your mouth, it will make you speechless. May cause the color of the lips to come back

In terms of fortune, this salary falls on the seat, so it is forbidden for others to borrow money or accept guarantees. Do not gamble and invest illegally or infringe on the copyright of others because this opportunity will have the right to jail as a dividend. You should also refrain from entering stocks and other investments during this period.

Monsoons are affecting the workplace. Maintaining positive relationships with those around you is essential. And don't forget about customers who require regular contact.

The family fortune is not always kind. Because this month's planets orbit the chains and stars.

You must be cautious that no one in your home is injured in an accident, and there is a risk of senior relatives mourning.

You are more likely to become ill from food poisoning, and you must be cautious of accidental blood injuries while traveling.

In terms of love, it is forbidden to meddle in other people's affairs because it will lead to arguments.

The fate of relatives and friends collides with the fate of dangerous companion stars. The best approach is to try to leave a gap before being duped into trouble.

Support Days: 1 Nov., 5 Nov., 9 Nov., 13 Nov., 17 Nov., 21 Nov., 25 Nov., 29 Nov.
Lucky Days: 4 Nov., 16 Nov., 28 Nov.
Misfortune Days: 7 Nov., 19 Nov.
Bad Days: 10 Nov., 22 Nov.

Month 11 in the Rabbit Year (7 Dec 23 - 5 Jan 24)
This month's horoscope still can soar, so the path is relatively easy. Previous challenges have been overcome. On this occasion, you should rush to produce results and make sales, keeping in mind that not bragging about your abilities will be a threat. You should also know what to give to the appropriate person and how to behave appropriately. This will assist you in remaining mindful and maintaining a positive image. Have patience and patience in both anger and adversity, perseverance, and the ability to analyze every work. Finally, the wisdom to know should be thoroughly understood. This will assist you in turning things around even during the monsoons.

Salary prospects are bright, cash inflows will continue to flow in both directions, and there are still many positive investment channels, so this is an excellent opportunity.

In terms of work, despite the damage, the results appear to be functional. As a result, you should pay more attention, be more diligent, and make continuous sales; your income will increase.

This month's family is visited by auspicious wealth. It's another month when you might get some good news from your family.

As for the blossoming and sweet love, there will be an opportunity to join the journey to create understanding and add sweetness to each other.

This month's health is excellent. Aches and pains in the body are reduced.

Relatives and friends, on the other hand, will benefit from trade advice.

During this time, starting a new job, entering into joint ventures, or investing in various investments will yield usable returns.

Support Days: 3 Dec., 7 Dec., 11 Dec., 15 Dec., 19 Dec., 23 Dec., 27 Dec., 31 Dec.
Lucky Days: 10 Dec., 22 Dec.

Misfortune Days: 1 Dec., 13 Dec., 25 Dec.
Bad Days: 4 Dec., 16 Dec., 28 Dec.

Amulet for The Year of the Pig

"Fu Lu Shou (God of fortune and long life)"
This year, those born in the Year of the Pig should establish and worship sacred objects. "Fu Lu Shou (God of fortune and long life)" to improve one's fortune. By placing it on a desk or cash register, you are asking Him for wisdom to do the right thing. prosperity and happiness to you and your family

(Take note of the direction in which the sacred object should be placed.) It is visible at the end of your life cycle.)

In the Department of Advanced Feng Shui, chapter one talks about the gods who will come down and reside in the annual Mi Keng (House of Destiny). which is the god that can inspire both you and the blame for the destiny that year When this is the case, worshiping to enhance your luck with the gods who come down to reside in the same year of your birth is considered to be the most beneficial and affecting you to rely on the prestige of that deity. Help protect your destiny while your destiny is in decline and misfortune is alleviated. At the same time, I would like to wish you a blessing to help inspire a smooth business venture and bring prosperity to you and your family.

Those born in the Year of the Pig or Mi Keng (Ruan Destiny) are in the zodiac of Hai, though this year appears to be auspicious overall. Good luck to you, but there is a murderous star in their destiny that harasses them all together. Fate must be careful not to miss the other person, be careful not to be deceived, or you will be spoiled until you realize it. Because the business, business, and finances are quite volatile, up and down, you should exercise caution before making any investment. As for the family, they must be cautious of thieves and accidents in the dark. Health may not be as good as it once was. Headaches, insomnia, and nausea are common complaints. You should relax because you are not stressed. Avoid accidents that could result in injury, bleeding, or rubber out. If you want to boost the auspicious things so that the results are clear. You should place sacred objects around your home and wear amulets. "Fu Lu Shou" (God of Luck, Wealth, and Age) asks the three gods for the power of prestige to help eliminate various types of dangers and losses. That will happen throughout the year. Only good fortune, wealth, and prosperity come to fate.

"Fu Lu Shou" is a symbol that represents the three Saint Deities in the Poi Xian process, also known as the Eight Successors. It is the ultimate auspicious blessing that will aid in promoting the destiny to be complete in all that he desires. "Fu" is derived from the word "Fuka" (Left Goddess), which means merit, luck, power, honor, stability, and wealth. "Lu" from "Hong Lu" (middle god) means fortune and wealth, full of wealth, that is, with consumables, glasses, silver rings, and full of family and wealth, having children, and a good life partner. And it is used by some people. "Shou" is derived from "Xiang Shou" (right angle), which means longevity and good health.

Those born in the Year of the Pig should also wear an auspicious pendant. "Fu Lu Shou" (God of Luck, Wealth, and Age) around your neck or carry it with you when traveling both near and far. so that your destiny is blessed with abundant wealth Both business and trade are prospering and advancing. A happy family all year results in greater efficiency and productivity, faster than ever before.

Good Direction: Northwest, Southwest, and East
Bad Direction: Southeast
Lucky Colors: Black, Blue, and Gray.
Lucky Times: 03.00 – 06.59, 13.00 – 14.59, 19.00 – 20.59.
Bad Times: 09.00 – 10.59, 15.00 – 16.59.